DATE DUE

AUG 03 2009			
GAYLORD			PRINTED IN U.S.A.

SandCastle™
Let's Measure

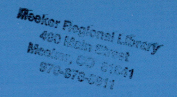
WHAT in the WORLD is an OUNCE?

Mary Elizabeth Salzmann

Consulting Editor, Diane Craig, M.A./Reading Specialist

ABDO
Publishing Company

Published by ABDO Publishing Company, 8000 West 78th Street, Edina, Minnesota 55439.
Copyright © 2009 by Abdo Consulting Group, Inc. International copyrights reserved in all countries.
No part of this book may be reproduced in any form without written permission from the publisher.
SandCastle™ is a trademark and logo of ABDO Publishing Company.

Printed in the United States.

Editor: Pam Price
Curriculum Coordinator: Nancy Tuminelly
Cover and Interior Design and Production: Colleen Dolphin, Mighty Media
Photo Credits: AbleStock, BananaStock Ltd., Colleen Dolphin, Shutterstock
Illustrations: Colleen Dolphin

Library of Congress Cataloging-in-Publication Data

Salzmann, Mary Elizabeth, 1968-

 What in the world is an ounce? / Mary Elizabeth Salzmann.

  p. cm. -- (Let's measure)

 ISBN 978-1-60453-167-1

 1. Volume (Cubic content)--Juvenile literature. 2. Measurement--Juvenile literature. 3. Weights and measures--Juvenile literature. I. Title.

 QC104.S355 2009

 530.8'13--dc22

                2008005485

SandCastle™ books are created by a professional team of educators, reading specialists, and content developers around five essential components—phonemic awareness, phonics, vocabulary, text comprehension, and fluency—to assist young readers as they develop reading skills and strategies and increase their general knowledge. All books are written, reviewed, and leveled for guided reading, early reading intervention, and Accelerated Reader® programs for use in shared, guided, and independent reading and writing activities to support a balanced approach to literacy instruction. The SandCastle™ series has four levels that correspond to early literacy development in young children. The levels are provided to help teachers and parents select appropriate books for young readers.

SandCastle Level: Transitional

Emerging Readers
(no flags)

Beginning Readers
(1 flag)

Transitional Readers
(2 flags)

Fluent Readers
(3 flags)

SandCastle™ would like to hear from you! Please send us your comments or questions.

sandcastle@abdopublishing.com

www.abdopublishing.com

OUNCE

An ounce is a unit of measurement. Ounces are used to measure weight. A slice of bread weighs about 1 ounce.

When you know how much an ounce is, you can find out how heavy something is.

The abbreviation for ounce is oz.

1 ounce is the same as 1 oz.

←bathroom scale

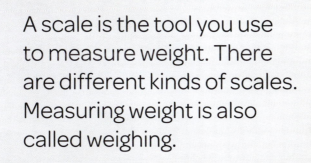

A scale is the tool you use to measure weight. There are different kinds of scales. Measuring weight is also called weighing.

kitchen scale

ROBERT CAN MEASURE!

Robert is going on vacation with his family.

He weighs the toys he is taking on the trip.

First Robert weighs
his stuffed bear.
It weighs 4 ounces.

Then he weighs his toy robot. It weighs 1 ounce.

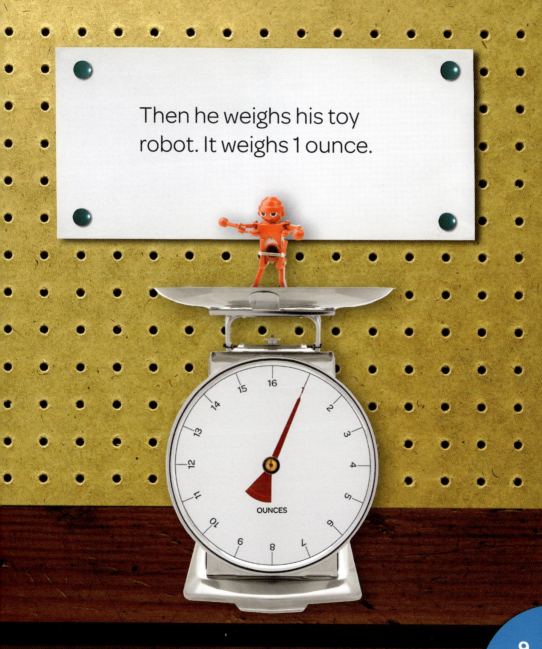

Robert weighs his truck. It weighs 2 ounces.

He weighs his baseball glove.
It weighs 7 ounces.

Robert weighs his dinosaur. It weighs 2 ounces.

Finally Robert puts all of the toys on the scale. They weigh 16 ounces!

$$\begin{array}{r} 4 \\ 1 \\ 2 \\ 7 \\ +\,2 \\ \hline 16 \end{array}$$

MEASURING EVERY DAY!

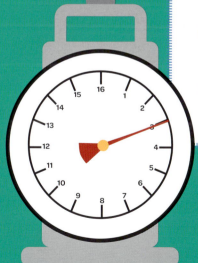

Keith measures the weight of his phone. It weighs 3 ounces.

Michael measures the weight of his soccer ball. It weighs 9 ounces.

Linda weighed the grapes at the grocery store before she bought them. The grapes weigh 14 ounces.

Paige needs 12 ounces of chocolate chips to make chocolate chip cookies. She weighs the chips on a scale to make sure she has the right amount.

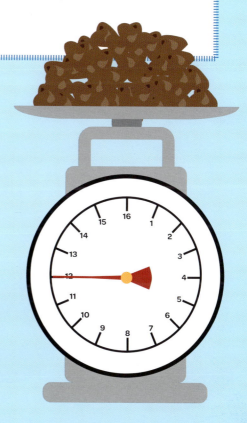

MEASURING IS FUN!

How many ounces does your favorite shirt weigh? What else can you measure in ounces?

LET'S MEASURE!

Which of these things is about one ounce?

(answer: AA battery)

MORE ABOUT MEASURING

Weight

16 ounces = 1 pound

Sometimes you use both pounds and ounces to weigh something.

The book weighs 1 pound and 4 ounces. This can also be written 1 lb. 4 oz.

GLOSSARY

abbreviation – a short way to write a word.

chocolate chip – a small piece of chocolate used in baking.

favorite – someone or something that you like best.

finally – last.

glove – a covering for the hand worn to play sports such as baseball and boxing.

grape – a small fruit that grows on a vine.

grocery store – a place where you buy food items.

measurement – a piece of information found by measuring.

scale – a tool used to measure weight.

unit – an amount used as a standard of measurement.

vacation – a trip away from home.